Into The Game

**Written By:
Kasey Peel**

**Copyright © 2024: Kasey Peel
All Rights Reserved. ISBN: 979-8-89324-423-6
Printed in the United States of America.**

No part of this publication shall be reproduced, transmitted, or sold in whole or in part in any form without prior written consent of the author, except as provided by the United States of America copyright law. Any unauthorized usage of the text without express written permission of the publisher is a violation of the author's copyright and is illegal and punishable by law. all trademarks and registered trademarks appearing in this guide are the property of their respective owners.

For permission requests, write to the publisher, addressed "attention: permissions coordinator," at the address below.

Amazon Book Publishing Center 420 Terry Ave N, Seattle, Washington, 98109, U.S.A

The opinions expressed by the author are not necessarily those held by Amazon Book Publishing Center.

Ordering information: quantity sales and special discounts are available on quantity purchases by corporations, associations, and others. for details, contact the publisher at Info@ Amazonbookpublishingcenter.com.

The information contained within this book is strictly for informational purposes. the material may include information, products, or services by third parties. As such, the author and publisher do not assume responsibility or liability for any third-party material or opinions. the publisher is not responsible for websites (or their content) that are not owned by the publisher. readers are advised to do their own due diligence when it comes to making decisions.

Amazon Book Publishing Center works with authors, and aspiring authors, who have a story to tell and a brand to build. Do you have a book idea you would like us to consider publishing? Please visit Amazonbookpublishingcenter.com for more information.

Contents

Chapter One: Getting Started 5
Chapter Two: DLT- Blockchain and Hashgraph 7
Chapter Three: Types of Coins and Tokens 10
Chapter Four: What to Look For 14
Chapter Five: Tips and Tricks for Beginners 17
Chapter Six: Funds Working For You 22

Chapter One: Getting Started

Hey, before we dive into the game of crypto, I just wanted to say this is one avenue of info/knowledge. It's not financial advice of any kind, just information and knowledge I've accumulated over the past few years.

"Money no longer has to be the root of all evil.
Money can be the seed of all possibilities."

We must learn how to take care of it, where to plant it, and what to do when planted.

This book was to give the readers that sense of understanding. To get to the point where learning and applying knowledge and skills becomes easy. It comes as a joyful journey and not a taunting setup for failure.

My journey started during COVID, when we continued to work and grow beyond survival means. I began to do research and explore ways to make money. When I discovered the crypto world, it took me many hours to grasp everything I needed. Even when I got the hang of it, I was open to learning more and more to avoid any possible mistakes—the extensive research and willingness to learn added value to my expertise and experience.

My reflections on what was right and what could go wrong broadened my horizons towards crypto. I continued to learn and apply the information that came along.

It's not an end-all-be-all; this game is constantly changing and growing. Be sure to continue your learning even after you have read this eBook. Also, while you read this eBook, it's always good to cross-check parts to see if I provided the most up-to-date information. There will always be risk when trading and investing in projects and companies. Please use your discernment when investing and trading; only risk what you are comfortable losing. With that being said, I hope your journey in this game is filled with insights and expansion, both internally and externally.

Let's get started!

Chapter Two: DLT- Blockchain and Hashgraph

Before jumping into the types of tokens/coins to invest in, let's talk about the Distribution Ledger Technologies in Cryptocurrency trading - the Blockchain and Hashgraph. Here's what you need to know about them:

Blockchain Technology:

Imagine a giant, transparent, and unchangeable Distributed Ledger Technology that records all transactions and activities. This ledger is not controlled by any single entity but is distributed among many computers worldwide. Each transaction or activity is grouped into a "block" and added to the "chain" of previous blocks, hence the name blockchain.

Here's the exciting part: Because the blockchain is decentralized and transparent, it promotes trust and security. No one can alter or delete any information once it's added to the blockchain. It's like having a public record that everyone can see and verify.

This revolutionary technology eliminates the need for intermediaries, such as banks or governments, to validate transactions. It allows for secure and direct peer-to-peer interactions, making processes faster, more efficient, and potentially more inclusive.

Blockchain is like a digital superpower that keeps track of transactions and activities, ensuring transparency and security for everyone involved. It's like having a global, tamper-proof database that anyone can access anywhere, anytime.

Hashgraph Technology:

Imagine a group in a room wanting to make a unanimous decision but not trusting each other completely. They want to find a fair and efficient way to agree on things and keep track of their choices.

In comes hashgraph technology, which is like a super-smart conversation manager. It allows everyone in the room to talk and share their opinions, but in a way that ensures fairness, accuracy, and security.

Here's how it works: Everyone in the room has a unique "hash" representing their opinion or decision. Whenever someone shares their hash with the group, the technology combines and analyzes all the hashes to determine the most popular opinion or decision.

But it doesn't stop there! Hashgraph also keeps track of the order in which the hashes are shared, creating a chronological "graph" of the conversation. This graph helps everyone see the history of decisions and ensures they remain unedited.

The most intriguing thing about hashgraph is that they're incredibly fast and efficient, with an average speed of 250 to 500,000 transactions per second. It can handle thousands of conversations simultaneously and keeps everyone in sync, even if some people are unreliable or try to disrupt the process.

In simpler terms, hashgraph technology is like a brilliant conversation manager that helps a group of people make decisions fairly and securely. It keeps track of opinions, ensures accuracy, and prevents tampering while being quick and efficient. It's like having a trustworthy and efficient secretary for group decision-making.

Hashgraph is a more sophisticated technology than blockchain. However, this does not imply that it will replace blockchain. There are still initiatives that can use blockchain more effectively than Hashgraph. Given that Hashgraph is privately held, adoption is gradual.

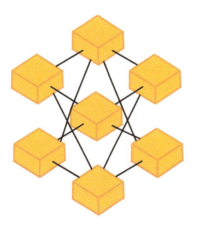
BLOCKCHAIN

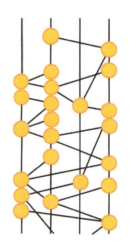
HASHGRAPH

Chapter Three: Types of Coins and Tokens

By now, you must be well-acquainted with the technology behind Crypto Trading, so it's time to talk about THE COINS.

When you dive into Crypto trading, you will encounter new coins almost daily. Coins that show incredible growth and top the market are critical and challenging to bid on. We have coins that are layer ones and twos.

Currently, bitcoin is the top dog, meaning the market usually moves with Bitcoin; it drives when the price will go up for top coins, which can be seen on websites like coin-market cap. I'll say the 1-5, then after bitcoin and those coins move. Then we get into something called alt season, which refers to all other coins. The coins that are considered alts can have different use cases and categories. As well as Bitcoin and the current top coins. Here are the types of coins and what they are about.

Coin vs Token

 A blockchain networks native asset

 Application built upon a coin's technology

 One coin per blockchain network

 Innumerbale tokens per blockchain network

 Uses a consensus mechanism for validation

 Relies on the native coin's consensus mechanism

1. **Bitcoin and Altcoins:** Bitcoin was the first and most well-known cryptocurrency. Altcoins refer to all other cryptocurrencies besides Bitcoin and coins such as Ethereum, Solana, BNB, and many more. Fun fact: coins like Bitcoin run their blockchain, while tokens(stable coins) like Tether rely on existing blockchains.

2. **Stablecoins:** Stablecoins are cryptocurrencies designed to have a stable value by pegging their price to a specific asset, such as a fiat currency (e.g., USD) or a commodity (e.g., gold). Examples include Tether (USDT), USD Coin (USDC), and Dai (DAI).

   So, let's say you see a stablecoin pegged to USD. Its price will be set to one dollar. The price usually won't go any lower than ninety-nine cents. Then, there was a story where a stable coin was de-pegged. You can look up the story of Terra Luna to learn more.

3. **Utility Tokens:** Utility tokens are cryptocurrencies that provide access to a specific product or service within a blockchain ecosystem. They are often used for decentralized applications (DApps) and can have various functionalities within their respective platforms. It means you will see these coins tackling world issues, like how XDC is helping digitize all world documents/assets. Or how the utility of HBAR lies in its ability to facilitate transactions, enable network resource allocation, provide governance rights, and foster participation in the Hedera Hashgraph ecosystem. It plays a vital role in the operation and growth of the network and serves as a fundamental component of the Hedera Hashgraph platform. These utility cryptocurrencies serve as the native cryptocurrency of their network and provide various utility functions within their ecosystem.

4. **Security Tokens:** Security tokens represent ownership of a real-world asset, such as stocks, bonds, or real estate. These tokens are subject to security regulations and offer investors rights and benefits similar to traditional financial instruments. It's a pretty precarious category since the XRP lawsuit. Security tokens are not yet available to retail investors, but many

institutions are working to get them approved by regulators

5. Privacy Coins: Privacy coins focus on enhancing the privacy and anonymity of transactions. Examples include Monero (XMR), Zcash (ZEC), and Dash (DASH), which utilize different privacy-enhancing techniques. Their straightforward operation allows us to move transactions discreetly with more privacy protection regarding your online interactions.

6. Platform Tokens: Platform tokens are cryptocurrencies that power blockchain platforms and enable developers to build decentralized applications. Ethereum's Ether (ETH) is the most well-known platform token. These are also known as layer ones. These blockchain networks serve as the foundational layer of a decentralized system. These networks are designed to independently handle various functions, including consensus, transaction validation, and smart contract execution.

Layer one cryptocurrencies are typically characterized by their ability to operate as standalone networks with native tokens—the foundation other ecosystems can build. Layer ones need help with different aspects of their network, such as scaling or speed. So, there is also a category of cryptocurrencies that are referred to as layer 2s.

Layer two solutions in the crypto space refer to protocols or frameworks built on the existing layer one blockchain. Again, they aim to address scalability and transaction throughput issues by offloading some of the computational workload from the layer one blockchain. Layer two solutions can enable faster and more cost-effective transactions while benefiting from the security and decentralization of the underlying layer one blockchain.

7. Interoperability Tokens: Interoperability tokens facilitate seamless communication and value exchange between blockchain networks. Examples include Polkadot (DOT), Quant(QNT), and Cosmos (ATOM). These are the bridges and connectors of the different ecosystems/blockchain networks.

8. Meme coin: Meme coins are created from something like a famous person's dog or movie. These coins are heavily influenced by the community gravitating towards the projects and their reach. It does not have utility in most cases. Some will use profits to help NGOs and Charities. Usually, this type of crypto concerns the community's hype and who backs it.

9. Non-Fungible Tokens (NFTs): NFTs are unique digital assets representing ownership or proof of authenticity of a specific item, such as artwork, collectibles, or virtual real estate. They are typically built on blockchain platforms like Ethereum. Sometimes, you can have an NFT that will produce a token that is a part of the NFT but not pegged to the NFT.

These are just a few examples and descriptions of different types of coins. The cryptocurrency landscape continuously evolves, with new types and categories emerging. It's critical to conduct thorough research and due diligence before engaging with any specific cryptocurrency or investment opportunity. Diversification may provide you with an overall harmony between projects that work well together even though they are in different categories of blockchain.

I hope this chapter gave you a comprehensive insight into the different types of coins.

For more information, you can also visit the website https://coinmarketcap.com/

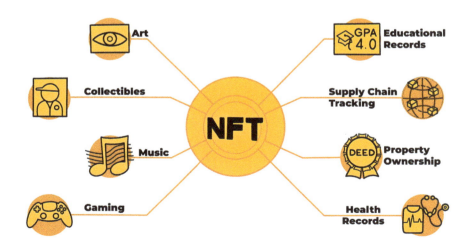

Chapter Four: What to Look For

When it comes to a project to invest in, there are a lot of factors that are at play. It can be overwhelming to anticipate if the project will succeed or flop. Some perspectives give you a clear guideline on differentiating between projects with solid promise and those that appear slightly hysterical. This mindset can be used in long or short-term holdings.

In my research era, I came across a "Five-rule" guide to help me recognize projects worth my time and money. Here's how it goes:

1. **Who is the team, and are they reliable?**

Meaning, are they public? Or have social media accounts? Can you find their pictures and the history of their story? Where can you learn about them?

2. **Who is backing them?**

Partnerships and investors play a crucial role in the success of any project. When influential entities like Microsoft or Visa invest, it signals a strong potential for success, as these smart money investors are selective and strategic, ensuring they see value and advantage before committing. Similarly, the involvement of celebrities, though sometimes perceived as less significant, can still bring substantial liquidity and influence. The backing of a famous individual can elevate the project's profile, driving both price and future development.

When every day people come together for a project they believe in—whether it's meme coins or the GameStop stock phenomenon—a strong and active community can significantly drive up the price. This collective effort boosts value and opens up new opportunities for the project's expansion and growth. The synergy of a dedicated community, combined with strategic partnerships and influential backers, can transform potential into tangible success.

3. What does the project have to offer?

This question helps you understand the project and what it offers the world. You can always check the roadmaps and allowlist on a project's website. So let's say you have a coffee shop, ok, but what does your coffee shop have that stands out among the others? You allow dogs to come and just be. These crypto projects need to be detailed with proof of what they provide for space and change in the world. You have specific cryptos that aim to change the financial system, making it faster and more cost-efficient than ever to transfer funds from person to person. And bank to banks. They are solving issues and challenges of the developing world and its systems.

4. What are the project's long and short-term goals and vision?

Are they a company that values the long-term dream they have in mind regarding the project as a whole? Do they have plans that show the integrity and drive of the project? A growth mindset helps ensure that the company and its project work hard and always dance between expansion and balance.

5. "Unicorn" or specialties of the project.

In the cryptocurrency market, a unicorn project is a privately owned venture valued at over one billion dollars. The term 'unicorn' depicts the rarity of such profitable businesses in cryptocurrency while just being in their developmental stage.

This area covers anything from knowing the CEO to the company's market share and sometimes gross and net income. To have a patent on something allows the "unicorns" to get ahead in their area of the game.

Again, these are five perspectives to consider when deciding which cryptocurrency project you want to make part of your portfolio. However, it would help if you did not confine your horizons, so allow yourself not to stop here but to apply and expand these even more.

Chapter Five: Tips and Tricks for Beginners

First and foremost, if you intend to invest in cryptocurrency, you must ensure your funds are in order. That involves having a backup fund, indebtedness that you can manage, and, most importantly, a diverse portfolio of investments. Your cryptocurrency investments can become another component of your portfolio, perhaps contributing to a higher return on investment.

Here are some more pointers to be taken into consideration:

1. Token circulation/spread:

For the spread of token holdings, you usually can see this on the project's website. It should have a healthy ratio of who holds what percentage of tokens. If the devs hold much of the supply, they can dump it on people once the price increases. I am not saying it always happens, but it is something to watch for. It also gives buyers and sellers a good impression of actual token circulation.

Sometimes, you have projects that release all tokens at once; some will gradually unlock more for the public as time goes on. Sometimes, there is a maximum supply of tokens, which means that's all there ever will be. Some projects are making more tokens. Some projects will burn their tokens when the supply is extensively high. You see this in most of the meme coins. It's usually done to make the token more attractive because the supply is decreasing. Token circulation is important for maintaining liquidity, price stability, network effects, token utility, and market perception. It contributes to the overall health and success of a blockchain ecosystem.

2. Market Cap:

It speaks on the valuation of the project. It's something to look out for because the market cap measures a company's or cryptocurrency's overall value. It is calculated by multiplying the current price per unit by the total number of units in circulation. Market cap helps investors determine the size and worth of a company or cryptocurrency relative to others. Also, high market cap assets often attract more attention from investors. A larger market cap suggests higher liquidity, stability, and market acceptance. Investors may view holdings with higher market caps as more attractive due to their perceived lower risk and higher potential for growth.

But remember, a small new project can have great partnerships and a great idea, and the market cap is much lower than many other cryptos. Once people become aware of the company and funnel in, the market cap will reflect higher as the price increases. So, high market caps attract investors, but one must have a point of view when considering the trends in market cap. You can see the potential benefits of projects with lower market caps. The market cap alone does not give a complete picture of an asset's value or potential. Yet, you will hear a lot in the space, so I thought I'd also factor it in.

3. Narratives and News:

Keeping yourself updated on the trends can help bidirectionally. If you see the news concerning taxes or the economy, this can put some tokens/projects in pullback mode, and the price will decrease. Or the opposite can happen; that's why being mindful of the news is important. Do your research and cross-reference the news you gather to give you a sound understanding of what's going on.

A crypto narrative is a theme or story that influences cryptocurrency investment and trading preferences. Trending crypto narratives may be characterized by the growing popularity of a specific set of cryptos, driven by greater adoption and vigorous blockchain activity.

People will start fearing missing out and throwing money into projects because of up-and-coming trends. Or, again, the opposite can happen, and the narrative of a specific market group or project can be hit with something that can rock the boat, speak. You can find news and narratives all over the internet; that's why it's important as you read and do your research. To not just follow one channel or website. Take notes, yes, but look around more.

Cross-referencing and seeing both sides of a story will give you a considerable advantage in your plans. It also means staying up to date on what your investments are doing, not just learning all this to buy and leave things alone. You can be balanced; you don't have to check every day if you do not want to. It's important to see what's happening with your investment projects and companies. To keep up to date is to protect and have clarity within your investments as your present and future choices.

4.   ICOs (Initial Coin Offerings) and Launchpads:

ICOs and launchpads may be risky, but they can be a great way to get on the ground floor of a new and upcoming project/token. These happen for many reasons, such as global reach. Only vetted investors and people with money could invest in startups or early projects. Now, things are different, allowing anyone who knows to invest in these upcoming projects. For launchpads, sometimes you'll have to do some things to be available to gain access to the project's launch, such as staking, which I'll explain in the upcoming chapter. Still, most of the time, it's about knowing the date of the ICOs and having a certain minimum of funds to invest.

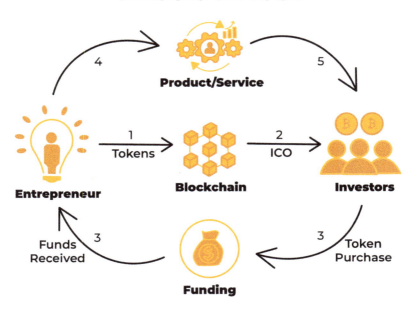

Another reason it is an interesting angle to look at is because of community building. This allows you to see who's coming together for this new project and how active the new community is. The company can gain liquidity and not use its capital to build its project, allowing more expansions to play out. Again, this also means when the project goes into the open market and on exchanges, you will have gotten in when the price was lower—potentially realizing gains much faster than waiting until the token was listened to on exchanges.

The same goes for launchpads. It is important to note that while ICOs and launchpads offer significant potential benefits, they also come with risks. Investors should conduct thorough due diligence and assess the project's team, technology, roadmap, and regulatory compliance before participating in any ICO, as stated earlier in this chapter.

So, as you decide your strategies to invest in projects, long or short-term, you can use these perspectives and angles to make clear choices without mindlessly going into the markets. You can apply these guidelines and use discernment to make the best out of this crypto game. Going into a project you truly believe in and enjoy is never truly a loss. As you understand the game more and gain experience, you will find perspectives and angles to go from. You'll learn what works and what doesn't work for you, and by strategizing your game plan, you can surely excel in crypto trading.

Chapter Six: Funds Working For You

So, the following chapter will be what you can potentially do with your accumulated tokens/coins. It's important to note the difference between the places you can hold your tokens. Before we dive into things, you can do with your tokens so that they work for you and provide even more value and potential profit.

So, let's start with exchanges like Coinbase, crypto.com, and Gemini. These are apps/platforms. You can create accounts with them and buy, sell, and hold your assets. Its pros are that it's easy to access your assets, and if you want to sell, they have a function that allows transfer right to the bank. You can also earn interest and stake certain tokens on the platform, which is easier to access. A risk is if the exchange goes bankrupt, as we have seen with FTX, or they get sued. Your funds get lost or frozen, resulting in you waiting a long time to access your assets/tokens. Or completely losing all the funds you have invested. Also, these websites and apps undergo maintenance, which can slow or shut down features and access to your tokens. If you want to swap tokens or move funds around, you won't be able to until maintenance is done.

Hot wallets are wallets you can download onto your desktop or phone. Storing your tokens in these types of wallets makes it possible to use platforms to work with staking, swapping, and yield farming. It provides you with a code to which only you have access; if you lose that code, you won't be able to get access to your tokens. Yet, it provides greater security against specific threats than having it on exchanges. This is your funds, so you won't have to wait to take out your money. These types of wallets are still online for the most part and come with some risk. Some of the examples include Trust Wallet, Exodus, and MetaMask.

Cold wallets are usable USB base drives to store your tokens. It also comes with codes and is completely offline until you go online and plug in the USB. Your tokens are safe if you don't lose the actual USB or code. However, as I have seen, these types of wallets are still updating. Again, the crypto game is expanding so rapidly that cold wallets do not support a lot of crypto tokens. Please do your research to find out if the cold wallet you'll buy supports the token you wish to store.

Now that you know what types of wallets you can choose, you know where to put your tokens. Here are some things you can do with your tokens to gain even more potential profit and allow the money to work for you.

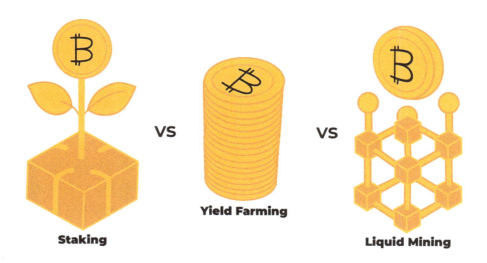

Staking:

Staking is the process of holding and actively participating in a blockchain network by locking up a certain amount of your tokens as collateral. By doing so, stakers contribute to the network's security, consensus mechanism, and overall functioning. In return for their participation, stakers are rewarded with additional cryptocurrency tokens.

Proof of Stake (PoS):

Staking is commonly associated with the Proof of Stake consensus mechanism, an alternative to the traditional Proof of Work (PoW) mechanism used in cryptocurrencies like Bitcoin. In PoS, validators are chosen to create new blocks and secure the network based on the number of coins they hold and are willing to "stake" or lock up as collateral. Token Lock-up, participants usually need to lock up their cryptocurrency for a specific period. This lock-up period can vary depending on the blockchain network and the specific staking requirements. During this period, the staked tokens are not readily available for trading or transferring, but they can still be utilized to secure the network. You can usually find where to stake/lock up tokens on the project's website. You can also see how long you would like to stake/lock up tokens if they give you the option.

Network Security:

Participants help secure and maintain the network's integrity by staking cryptocurrency. Validators are incentivized to act honestly and follow the network's rules, as they risk losing their staked funds if they behave maliciously or violate the consensus rules.

Earning Rewards:

Stakers receive rewards for their participation in the network. These rewards are typically in the form of additional cryptocurrency tokens. The reward distribution can vary depending on the specific blockchain protocol, but it is generally proportional to the amount of cryptocurrency staked. Staking can provide a passive income stream for token holders, especially if they compound their rewards by restaking them.

Governance and Voting Rights:

Some staking systems give participants governance and voting rights. Stakers can have a say in the decision-making process for protocol upgrades, parameter changes, and other governance matters. The voting power is often proportional to the amount of cryptocurrency staked, giving more influence to those with larger stakes.

Staking Pools:

Staking can sometimes require a significant amount of cryptocurrency to participate effectively. Stocking pools exist to overcome this barrier, where multiple users combine their resources to stake and collectively earn rewards. By pooling their funds, participants can increase their chances of being selected as validators and share the rewards proportionally.

Staking has gained popularity as a way for crypto holders to participate in blockchain networks actively, earn rewards, and contribute to network security and governance. However, it is essential to consider the risks involved, such as potential slashing (penalties for malicious behavior), market volatility, each staking protocol's specific rules and requirements, and the regulations for where you currently live. Be mindful of these risks so you know when to put your tokens into a cold wallet or move them out of staking and into stable coins or a hot wallet. And make the best choice for yourself regarding what to do with tokens/assets.

Yield farming:

Yield farming is a specific activity within the DeFi space. It involves using various DeFi protocols and strategies to maximize returns on cryptocurrency holdings. Yield farming participants provide liquidity to decentralized exchanges

(DEXs) or lending platforms and earn rewards through additional tokens.

How Liquidity Pool Works

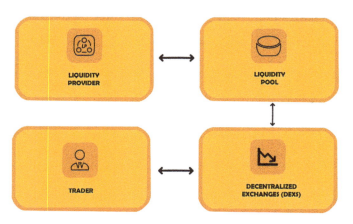

1. Liquidity Provision: Yield farmers provide liquidity to decentralized exchanges or lending platforms by depositing their cryptocurrency assets into smart contracts. This liquidity enables trading and borrowing activities within the DeFi ecosystem.

2. Yield Optimization: Yield farmers employ different strategies to optimize their returns. They may move their funds between different protocols to take advantage of higher yields or utilize complex strategies involving lending, borrowing, and leveraging to increase their potential earnings.

3. Token Rewards: In return for providing liquidity, yield farmers receive additional tokens as rewards. These rewards are often in the form of governance tokens specific to the DeFi protocol or platform in which they participate. These tokens can be sold, staked, or used within the protocol for voting and governance purposes.

Yield farming can be highly lucrative, but it also carries risks. The DeFi space is still relatively new and rapidly evolving, making it important for participants to thoroughly research and understand the protocols they engage with. Risks include Smart Contract Vulnerabilities, impermanent loss (potential loss when providing liquidity), market volatility, and potential scams or rug pulls.

And that concludes the end of this eBook; we spoke about different categories of cryptocurrencies. And what they do in the space; we discussed risk and diversity.

I have shed light on perspectives that will help you decide what to look for when investing in a project—different places to hold your tokens and ways to engage with crypto and blockchain spaces.

I hope this was an informative read and would help you kickstart your crypto adventure.

Thanks for reading!

Milton Keynes UK
Ingram Content Group UK Ltd.
UKHW050030211024
449849UK00004B/10